JENNIFER REED

A JOURNEY OF TRAUMA, REDEMPTION & RECOVERY

THIS WORD CALLED LOVE

NAMES AND PLACES HAVE BEEN CHANGED TO PROTECT THE GUILTY!

Edited by Ina Newbury

Copyright © 2024 by Jennifer Reed

This book is memoir. It reflects the author's present recollections of experiences over time. Names, places, and some defining characteristics have been changed, some events have been compressed, and some dialogue has been recreated.

A JOURNEY OF TRAUMA, REDEMPTION & RECOVERY

THIS WORD CALLED LOVE

This book is dedicated to my many friends
who have made my life a joy, not even knowing
and realizing what was going on inside of me.
Their kindness will never go unnoticed.

It is also dedicated to one very special friend
that knew everything and never judged me.
Thank you for believing in me and helping me to believe in myself.
Thank you for giving me the courage to tell my story
and the courage to handle whatever kind of results it may bring.

I am affectionately dedicating to my
Lord and Savior Jesus Christ
for putting his hands on me throughout
these dark times of my life.
Without him, the healing from my past
would defintely not be a part of my future.

INTRODUCTION

Growing up as a little girl, I should have had the memories of playing dolls with my friends, family vacations, Vacation Bible Schools at my church, and spending special times with my grandparents. This was not the case - it was all pretty much the opposite. I told no one anything; I tried once but it failed. Fear of not knowing this was wrong, I kept it all inside. I was a good girl, so I did not understand why these things happened to me. What did I do to deserve this?

My life was tarnished, and I continued down the path of hurt. I went to church on most Sundays and talked to God alone. Fear and embarrassment kept me from reaching out for help.

To best describe my situation, I was like a pretty rose just like the one on the cover of my book. The thorns on that rose bush were there, permanently inside, ripping my heart and soul apart. You never know what someone is going through, even if they "seem" happy. I was dying inside.

CONTENTS

THIS
WORD
CALLED
LOVE

1
THE BEGINNING OF SEXUAL ABUSE

I was born to incredibly young parents. My mom was only fourteen when my brother was born, and when I was born twenty-two months later, she was sixteen and my dad nineteen. Today they call this "kids raising kids." So, my dad's parents were always involved helping raise us. My dad had a job as a machinist at night, and my mom stayed home learning how to be a mom. And since we lived right next door to my grandparents, Mom felt safe at night. Whenever she would get scared, my grandfather would come over and stay until my dad got home early in the morning.

I remember one summer night when we had no air conditioning but relied on attic fans and open windows to cool the house, my mom had been sitting in a chair by the window solving a crossword puzzle when she started screaming, waking me and my brother. She said someone was calling her name and telling her to open the door. She called my grandparents, and when my grandfather came, he looked all around but did not see anyone. He told us he would stay until our daddy got home just in case. He did this a lot anyway, so we were used to it. But something was not right that night. She said the voice sounded just like my grandpa's. I have often wondered if my grandfather was abusing my mother. Were the nights staying at my house all for his benefit? My mom was a beautiful young woman, and many men found her attractive. I have always wondered, because of what happened to me, if my grandfather did things to her.

I remember many good childhood memories of going to the zoo, the beach, and on mini vacations with the whole family. We never went anywhere without my grandparents. My brother and I were loved and cared for – that is, until I was seven years old, and sexual abuse began.

My brother and I spent many nights with my grandparents next door because my parents were young and liked to go out with their friends on the weekends. I will never forget the night it all began. We had all finished dinner and were watching TV in my grandparents' big living room. I remember sitting on my grandpa's lap when Mom and Dad got up to say goodnight. They were headed home and told us we could go with them or spend the night there. We both wanted to stay as we had countless times before. Grandpa said I could sleep with him, and my brother could use the guest room. That was good for me because I was often scared at night and did not like to be alone.

When we all went to bed, Grandpa and I talked and laughed a little before I began to fall asleep. I woke up to his fingers touching me and rubbing me in my privates. I was unsure why he was doing that, so I just rolled over on my belly, but he still managed to touch me and rub me there. I asked him why he was doing that, and he said he loved me and assured me that was what you do when you love your family. I was a little confused because my mom and dad had never done anything like that to me. He was my grandpa, and I did love him, but I could not understand what was going on. He told me to roll over on my side and cuddle up to him. And when he held me for a few minutes, I felt better. He told me to try to go back to sleep, but how could I? He put his penis between my legs and started moving back and forth, shaking the whole bed! Next thing I knew, I was WET all over! I did not like this, not at all! I wanted to get up and put on some dry pajamas, but he would not let me. He told me to just be quiet and go to sleep.

The next day was Sunday. We all went to church and came back to my grandparents' house for lunch. Mom and Grandma were frying chicken, and we were all going to watch the televised football game. My grandfather laid on the couch and asked me to come lay by him. NO! I did not want to! I did not want that to happen again with everybody there watching. So, I went over and crawled in the recliner with my daddy. My daddy never did things like that to me.

All the next week, I stayed at home in my own bed, but when the weekend arrived and my mom and dad were going out with friends, they planned for us to spend the night with my grandparents again. I knew that meant I would be sleeping with my grandpa again, so I tried to get my brother to switch and sleep with him, but he refused. It was just as well because I would be scared to sleep alone there anyway. I wanted to ask my grandmother if I had to do these things with my grandpa, but he told me not to talk to her about it because he said it would hurt her feelings if she thought he loved me more than her. That made no sense, but I was not about to hurt my grandma's feelings. So, I kept quiet.

As I began to fall asleep again, he did the same thing with his fingers but was a lot rougher than before, and it was painful! He told me he was sorry for hurting me, but if I crawled on top of him, it would be better. I tried to, but that thing was in the way! He tried to put it inside of me, but I cried, "That hurts!" It was too big! He stopped and just put it between my legs and bounced me up and down till I was all WET again. Was this love? I had never seen this before! I wondered, "Does he do this with my grandma?" I had so many questions, but I could not hurt my grandma's feelings by asking. I knew my grandpa loved me because he bought me anything I asked for. He had just recently bought me a horse. This went on for three years. Grandpa showed me every time I spent the night with him how much he loved me and kept buying me all sorts of stuff. I had come to accept that this was normal.

But when I was ten, he took it too far! He penetrated me, and it really, really hurt! I was crying real tears. He finally stopped – but not until I was WET again! The next day I could not go to the bathroom without a lot of pain, and it was hard for me to even walk. He told me not to tell Mom or Dad because he planned to tell them, but I had to agree with what he said, or we would both be in a lot of trouble. He told them I was walking the board fence at his house, and I fell straddling it. Momma checked me, but she asked no questions, and the incident was never again discussed.

Over the next few weeks, I got better, but when Grandpa did not try to love me again it confused me and made me sad because I thought it meant that he did not love me anymore. He assured me that he was sorry he hurt me, and we would love again soon. I went on for a few weeks in turmoil – afraid he did not love me but grateful he was not hurting me anymore.

After several weeks passed, my grandfather was using the tractor to build a dog pen for my daddy's coon hunting dogs. He knew I loved driving the tractor, so he asked me to come outside and help him with the project. Since my daddy was out there, I felt safe knowing he would not do anything to me in front of him. So, I went and jumped on his lap and helped him drive. As we got closer to finishing the project, my dad left to go inside, saying that he had not eaten all day and was hungry. And that was when it started. My grandfather pulled that thing out of his pants and told me to sit on it. I reminded him it really hurt and started crying. He told me he would just put it between my legs like before so it would not hurt me, and I did as he asked.

After it was over, he jumped off the tractor to straighten his pants and I accidentally bumped the gear into reverse and backed over the dog pen we had just built, smashing it to pieces. He was screaming and yelling at me to stop! He told me to get off the tractor, get in the house, and not come back out there. I was devastated; I had done everything he asked, and now he did not love me. When my dad saw the dog pen, he never asked any questions because he felt like that was the only reason for my emotional outburst.

Three or four weeks later, my grandpa was out bush hogging the weeds in our pasture and had a massive heart attack. He managed to get himself to the hospital in our small town but had another heart attack while he was there and passed away. Although I still could not understand the things he did to me, I was devastated by his death. And to this day I have never told anyone what he did. It was not until I got older that I realized it was sexual abuse and was very wrong.

My childhood has been forever tainted by these memories, and his abuse had a lasting, detrimental effect on my life. I got pregnant when I was fifteen because I believed I had to do whatever my boyfriend wanted to make sure he loved me. My dad would not allow me to keep the baby and made me get an abortion, even though that was a taboo subject in those days. And after a lifetime of being sexually active with many boyfriends and experiencing two failed marriages, the only good that came from them were my three sons. I love them with all my heart.

Life has not been easy as a single mom raising three boys on my own, but I have done it. There were times I did not know where our next meal was coming from, but God provided. I made a promise to myself that no one would ever abuse me again. And that vow played a crucial role in my life. I blame failed marriages and failed relationships on my childhood trauma and my inability to understand the difference between love and abuse.

When I wanted to give up, God
took my hand and told me to get up.

2

ABUSE VS. MARRIAGE

My first marriage began when I ran away from home with a guy I had only known for a couple of months. I did not believe my dad loved me because he was so hard on me. I was so confused about what real LOVE was – a confusion that stemmed back to my relationship with my grandpa. I believed if I was not having sex, I was not loved. So, I secretly packed my clothes, ran off with Bill, and called my dad three days later to tell him I was married and not coming home. He was devastated. He explained how badly I had hurt him and told me he did not want me to come home for a long time.

The only thing I knew about Bill was that he was a cowboy and he showed me every day that he loved me – the only way I knew love. But he was 21, had no job, and depended on his mom to take care of him. We lived in his mom's house, as she had remarried and moved in with her new husband. But she paid all our bills, and every week she took me to the grocery store to buy all our food. I knew this was not right.

Every time his mom came over, Bill would ask her for money, and then they would get into a big argument. One day when she told him to get a job because she was tired of supporting him, he hit her so hard she fell to the kitchen floor. I was screaming and crying, "Bill, please stop! How could you hit your own mom?" In response, he walked across the kitchen and slapped me!

The next morning, I got up and went out looking for employment. I needed to get out of that house, and I needed to make some money. I had to stop Bill from treating his mom so mean. She provided a place for us to live, paid all the bills, and fed us. I had to do my part! I found a job working as a switchboard operator for the local hospital on the night shift. I knew Bill would not like this idea, but we had no choice. So, he took me to work at three in the afternoon and picked me up at eleven at night. Things were going downhill; I was working, and he was not, and we fought about money all the time. Then he began showing up late to pick me up when I got off at night.

I was about to call my dad to ask if I could come home when I found out I was pregnant. I was convinced that I had to stay, and I tried over the next few months to make things better, but Bill was redheaded and extremely short tempered. He said ugly things to me as I gained weight with the baby and slapped me a couple of times. But through it all, I was determined to stay and have this baby.

When our son was born, things got better for a while. But the extra expense of diapers, formula, and other things needed for the baby caused more money problems. My mother-in-law was good to help, but she was in a new marriage, and her husband was getting exasperated by her spending, so that began to cause problems for her.

We began visiting my parents on the weekends, and my dad, who was proud of his new grandson, would always give us a little cash while we were there. One day he told me if I bush hogged his pasture, he would pay me $100. I agreed, and my dad and Bill sat and visited while I worked. I loved the tractor and drove it a lot as a child, and my dad knew that. But Bill decided it was time to leave before I was finished. He walked out to the pasture where I was and said, "Let's go!" I told him I would be through in a little bit, but he grabbed me by the arm and jerked me off the tractor, throwing me to the ground. My dad was quick to get there, and things got intense. We left and went home, but I knew I had to get away from this hot-tempered husband or he would seriously hurt me.

I found an excellent job about a week later paying a lot more than the hospital, and my dad sent me money to move out with my two-year-old son, and we did just that! But other than working, I stayed in the house with my son most of the time. Bill circled my house at night and stalked me at my new job during the day, so I was afraid to do much of anything outside the safety of my job or my home. But thankfully, Bill soon found a girlfriend and stopped coming around.

Meanwhile, I had met a new man at my new job who said he was divorced and had two little boys. I was beginning to be happy again, but I made the mistake of moving in with him shortly after we met. I needed financial help, and I thought this was my chance. I mistakenly took this attraction as love because he paid so much attention to me. I did not realize that it was the wrong kind of attention. I fell for it every time. It was not love but only lust. When would I learn? My childhood destroyed my future, and I did not know how to take control of my life. This relationship lasted only three months, and my son and I had to find a place to live again.

After several more months of staying home with my son most of the time, I was tired of having no life and decided to go out with some girlfriends who had invited me to go with them to a dance hall. I agreed, feeling that I needed some fun in my life right then. I met this man, and we danced all night long. At the end of the night, he asked me to go out with him the next night. He said we danced so well together we would come back the next night and do it again! I accepted, and the second night was as good as the first one. We danced the night away. Then it happened. I went home with him. Here we go again. LOVE – but the wrong kind. It was a pattern with me, and I did not know how to take charge and stop the cycle. I still blamed my grandfather. How long would I live this nightmare?

We dated for three months, but then one day I was so sick I could not go out with him that night. I went to the doctor the next day because I had thrown up so much, I thought I was dehydrated. Oh no! I was pregnant! Again! "Not now," I prayed. "This is not a good time." When he found out about the child, he asked me to marry him, and I accepted. But would this end the same way my other relationships ended? We certainly enjoyed dancing and we engaged in a lot of "LOVE," but was it really love?

Eight months passed, and I welcomed Caleb into this world. I could not be happier, and now my husband was a first-time dad! He was thrilled! He was five years younger than me and still a little immature for his age, but I was hoping that raising his son would grow him up. We could not stay in the dance halls all the time now! He had a wife, a stepson, and a new baby now, so things would have to be different. Times were stressed financially, but we were making it. Then I got pregnant again when Caleb was only six months old. How was I going to do this? And by the time James was three months old, I saw that our marriage was in trouble. He still wanted to go dancing all night and I had three kids at home. I knew I was headed for another failed relationship when he would leave me home at night to go out dancing. Some nights he came home, and sometimes he did not. This word called LOVE was ruining my life. I knew he was out there spreading his love to another woman! I stayed with him for another year and a half in an unhappy marriage only because I knew I could not make it on my own with three children. My husband was never home, but at least the kids and I had a place to stay. I would leave as soon as I could figure it all out.

When my two youngest babies were a year and two years old, I found a good paying job, rented a house, and moved out. It was hard financially but tight finances kept me at home with the kids because I had no money to go anywhere. Years passed as I worked hard to support my three sons. I did not trust men at all, and I hated the word *"love."* It brought too many childhood memories that I just could not clear from my mind. I know my childhood trauma affected me all through my life and caused a lot of confusion and pain. And besides that, the promise I made to myself that I would never experience sexual abuse did not come true, and the resulting pain has been unbearable.

When you have fought so hard to get back on your feet,
to talk to God, and to change your life,
do not go back to the life you were living.

3

JAIL...
PRISONER...
SEXUAL ABUSE...

As I nervously sat across the table from the seven men conducting my interview for the job, I would never have expected that I would someday be brutally assaulted sexually by three of them. I was interviewing for a secretarial position for their insurance company, and I was told that I would be working closely with these men individually on a day-to-day basis. After my history of assaulting the County Attorney's secretary in the Courthouse, these men wanted to make sure I was the right person for this job.

So, if you are asking yourself, *Why would a woman of my age march into the County Courthouse and attack the County Attorney's secretary in broad daylight?* I will need to give you a brief history to bring you up to date for the interview at the insurance company.

I was a twice-divorced mother of three beautiful sons. I was very independent and a hard worker. To begin with, I was working for an anesthesiologist in town and had been there a little over a year, when one day while sitting at my desk, two men with badges barged into my office and told me not to answer the phones and to open the patient filing cabinet for them, as they would be taking all the files with them. I told them I needed to call the doctor at the hospital before I could unlock the patient files. They agreed. He told me not to give them anything. He would be there as soon as he could. They got upset with me, changed the locks on the office door, and escorted me out. All they shared with me was that they were from the Medicare Fraud Unit, and this doctor was committing fraud with his billing records. If I had helped him, I would be in a lot of trouble too. I was so frightened! I billed Medicare based on what he gave me. I went home and heard nothing for three days. Finally, I received a telephone call from one of the representatives telling me that I was not in trouble, as I was only doing what the doctor asked me to do. But Medicare closed the office, and I was without a job, just that quickly.

It took weeks of searching to find a job, and times were hard. My parents paid for my utilities so my children and I would have a place to stay, and I wrote insufficient checks to grocery stores to feed my kids and insufficient checks for gas so I could continue looking for a job. My house was financed through FHA, and they helped me defer my house payments until I could find a job.

Finally, I landed a job as a data entry operator at Reiman Business Forms. The pay rate was good, but it took all I earned to pick up the bad checks I wrote plus the bank fees. Warrants were issued quicker than I could pick up the checks from the County Attorney's office. I was so embarrassed! One morning I called the County Attorney office to let them know I would be coming in on my lunch hour. I wanted to call ahead because I had just started this new job and could not be gone long. The secretary told me to be there a little before 12:00 because she left at noon. She said if I paid cash, it would only take about 10 minutes to take care of the bad check. I arrived at 11:45 a.m. by taking my lunch break a few minutes early, only to see her walking out the door. I asked her why she was leaving when she had agreed to wait for me. In a sarcastic tone she said she could leave when she wanted to. I begged her to please take care of me as I arrived earlier than I said I would. I could not wait till she got back because it would make me late getting back to my new job, and that would not be good. She flippantly replied, "I will be back at 1:00," and smiled as she walked past me.

I called my employer to tell him I would be late, as I had to take care of this matter, and he was not happy with me. The secretary arrived back at 1:00 like she said, but when I followed her into her office, I was not nice to her. My tone certainly reflected my anger. She walked over to me, shaking her finger in my face and admonishing me to change my tone or she would not take care of me at all. Well, she accidentally hit my nose with her finger, and that was all it took! I saw fire! I doubled up my fist and punched her in the nose. Now, to this day I have no idea how I connected with her nose, because she was at least five inches taller than me. I guess anger can make you do a lot of things you may not know you can do. All I remember after that was flying fists and hair getting yanked. The next thing I knew, the sheriff had a hold of my shirt collar and was informing me, "If you hit me, I *will* hit you back!" That calmed me down quickly.

I was taken downstairs, fingerprinted, and put in a holding cell. I was upset and crying, not sure what to do next, as I had never been in this kind of trouble before. The sheriff told me I had one call I could make. I called my daddy, but I could not even tell him what I had done because I was crying so hard, so the sheriff talked to him for me. My father, being the tough man he was, refused to post my bond to get me out of a jail. But the sheriff felt sorry for me and made a few calls around town, finding an attorney that would post my bond so I could get home to my kids. Of course, by this time it was too late to go back to work.

The next morning when I walked into the office, I saw all my personal belongings packed in a box on my desk and my supervisor waiting for me in her office. As I walked in, she angrily questioned, "Do you know what you have done? Do you know whose nose you broke at the courthouse?" Well as it turned out, she was the Reimen

Business Forms' plant manager's wife. I was fired immediately and escorted to my car by two security officers. Here I was again with no job! Thankfully, I had a final paycheck coming that would carry me through for a little while, and my dad had taken care of the rest of the bad checks. After refusing to get me out of jail, he did call in and take care of the checks for me.

Within two weeks I found another job as the secretary for the Chamber of Commerce in town. They liked me and felt that I would be great for the job. I did not disclose that I was still on probation for the assault which had been reduced to a Class B Misdemeanor since I had never been in trouble with the law, and I was praying they would not find out. But a few weeks after I was hired, the local newspaper printed an article about the Chamber of Commerce in which they announced me as the new secretary. The newspaper came out that morning, and that afternoon my boss called me to his office. He had received a call from someone; he would not tell me who, but he said I could not represent the Chamber of Commerce because I was on probation for assault. He sadly had no choice but to terminate me.

Here I was again with no job and such low morale. The only thing that kept me from falling into deep depression was that my three beautiful sons were watching me. I had to be strong and carry out my daily routine for them. I had to go on and be strong for them. But in my daily search for jobs, I only looked for ones that would keep me out of the public eye because I could not even hold my head up as I went about town for fear of being recognized and approached by the curious. I felt so much shame.

I finally found a job cleaning out rental houses and apartments when they were vacated. It was offered through a cleaning service, the money was adequate, and I did not have to be seen in public, so I considered it a win-win. But the job eventually turned into seven days a week with long hours, and my sons and I missed each other. My middle son is autistic, and our routine was blown with me working so many hours. He was acting out and experiencing depression because of my absence. I had to find another job because I could not stand to see him this way. I stuck a little money aside and quit this job as soon as I could.

I searched the newspaper daily for two weeks until I saw an ad for a secretary at an insurance company. It was an eight to five job and close to my home. I felt brave and helpless all at the same time as I updated my resume. I needed to be home with my boys as much as possible and this job was only five days a week, so I prayed and prayed this opportunity would turn out well. I mailed in the resume and waited. When seven days passed, I was ready to give up when I received a call to come in for an interview. I was as excited as I was scared. Would I get this job and then get fired again? Would they find out about the fight at the courthouse and fire me later? How many times would I have to go through this? But I scheduled the interview and went in. The agency manager and the other secretaries seemed to like me, and I was asked to come back for a second interview with all the insurance agents, as I would be working one on one with them daily. I agreed to come back, but that night I went into panic mode. Should I go ahead and tell them about the fight at the courthouse? Should I tell them about probation even though it was almost over? I did not sleep much that night but decided the best thing to do was to be up front and honest, even if it caused me not to get the job. By being open, perhaps I would not get fired later.

The interview began with each man facing me holding a pen and notepad to write down whatever I said. The first few questions were to ascertain if I had experience in the insurance field. I told them I had some – not a lot – but I was a fast learner and very eager to learn. My past employers came up as they noted I had moved from job to job. They all wanted to know why I never stayed with any job long. Here was my chance! I had decided to be up front, and I was. I explained in detail, beginning with the doctor's office all the way up through the Chamber of Commerce. I even explained the courthouse, the hot checks, and probation. No one said a word. I only got dead silence and blank stares, and I felt horrible. I had no idea whether I should get up and walk out or stay and take what was coming. Several of them asked questions about the incidents, so the interview was over an hour long. Finally, the agency manager asked me to step outside for a few minutes while they discussed my employment. It seemed like hours, but it was only fifteen minutes before they called me back in. The manager said they felt that I had been dealt a bad hand of cards, and they all wanted to give me a chance. I burst into tears in disbelief. Then the agency manager said I had to make him one promise before they hired me. I cried, "Sure! Absolutely! Anything," though I was not even sure of what he would ask. He went on to say that I would have to promise that I would never get mad and hit one of the other office secretaries I had met earlier. I could not hold back the tears or laughter as I said, "No, I will never lay a hand on anyone else my whole life. I have learned my lesson!" I knew God had answered my prayers. I had a job!

Little did I know that the worst trauma of my life was about to begin! I started my job on the following Monday and loved it, working full-time with Ellen, who had been there over ten years and showed me everything I needed to know. She was a little moody but that was nothing I could not handle. Another secretary, Susan, only worked half a day filing claims for the insured, and she trained me to do her job as well. I was especially nice to these ladies, as I was determined to make this work and was not sure what all they had been told about me.

After a few months, Susan's husband became extremely ill, and she had to quit and stay home to take care of him. And since I had exceeded expectations and excelled in my job, they gave me her responsibilities to add to mine. I knew I would be busy, but as the months passed, I was doing great.

The drama started the day I took a call from one of our insured clients who wanted to file a claim on his chicken coops. He said the tornado that came through the day before tore them all up, so

I went into the agent's office to pull his file and inform the agent that he was filing a claim. When I sat down at my desk to type the claim, I noticed that this man lived right down the road from me, and there had been no tornado or rain in our neighborhood. I said nothing to the insured, just filed the claim as he had asked. But I did approach his agent later that day and informed him that the client was my neighbor and there was no tornado. He told me to be quiet and mind my own business, so I did just that! A few days later, I received a phone call from a different client filing a remarkably similar claim. Now I knew things were not right! At the end of the day, I went in to speak with the agency manager about both claims, telling him I was not comfortable with what I was being asked to do. When I explained both claims to him, he told me he was already aware of the problems and was working behind the scenes to get things straightened out. He told me to keep doing what I was doing and not say anything to anyone else. He told me not to worry – he had my back and would not let anything hurt me, assuring me that I would not be accused of anything. This went on for several months, and I was worried because I knew we were doing things that were wrong and illegal. This wonderful job I was so happy with was turning into a nightmare. And it soon did!

Then on September 13, 1990 (it was my dad's birthday, so I will never forget!), I was at my desk working when suddenly the front door flew open and in marched eight men with badges and guns. They identified themselves as private investigators and the local police. One investigator, Mike with International Insurance Investigations, ordered me and Ellen not to answer the phones. He told us that the phones were tapped and that he was spearheading the investigation into fraudulent claims being filed through our office. They walked down the hall into the Insurance Adjuster's office and fired him immediately. The police escorted him out the back door while they started boxing up everything in his office and carrying it out to the police cars, cleaning out everything but his desk and chairs.

They hung a microphone from the ceiling in front of a chair and called me in to sit there as they recorded everything I said. Police officers lined the wall. I was informed by Mike that the police officers were prepared to arrest me on the spot and CPS officials were standing by to take my children if I did not fully cooperate with this investigation. I was scared to death! My thoughts were racing. "Take my children? Why?" I had done nothing wrong. I had informed the agency manager what I saw, and he told me to keep doing it. This nightmare I was working in was intensifying!

The police officer came forward and asked me to state my full name. He then told me he knew of my three sons and called them by name, gave their ages, the name of their school, and their teachers' names. I was crying and trembling by now. Terrified was not even the word to describe the way I felt. All I wanted to do was to call my daddy. I knew he would tell me what to do. I knew he was in no shape to come to me, as he was suffering from lung cancer. I asked to call him, and they agreed as long as I did it in front of them. My daddy quickly told me to call a lawyer and not to trust them. But when I told them my daddy told me to call lawyer, they were furious and would not allow me to make that call. They said I had better tell them everything I knew about what was going on, or I would be there all night. I was not leaving until I cooperated. They did not care that I had kids at home with a babysitter. They did allow me to call my babysitter and ask her to stay late.

They took my picture and informed me that their plan was to put it on a badge under the title of International Insurance Investigator and present it to each agent, informing them that I had been working undercover for the past year and had caught them in the act. I believed they were really going to do this and knew I had to cooperate, even though my dad warned me not to trust them. I feared they would take my kids if I could not prove I had no part of this fraud. Finally, at eight pm, two of the investigators told me they would let me go home to my children if I came back in the morning and continued to tell them what I knew. They were on a fishing expedition, and I was the bait! They knew this fraud had been going on for several years, but until now they had no proof, so I was needed to provide the paper trail. They took me home in the police car and made me leave my car at the office because they intended to pick me up the next morning after my children left for school.

The next morning was rough. They made me go into the office of each agent while they sat at their desk and pull the files of all the insured clients I had filed insurance claims for. If looks could kill, I would have been dead that day. It took most of the day because there were so many files to collect. At the end of the day, three of the agents were told to clear their personal belongings out of their offices and not come back.

The following day was even harder. The insurance investigator, Mike, gave me a camera and compelled me to ride in their car with them to the agents' homes where I was told to take pictures of their homes, cars, and personal property. Mike said it was very apparent that these agents could not live these rich lifestyles by just selling insurance. Two of the agents came out and told me to leave before I got hurt. The others just watched from their windows.

I kept telling the investigator that these men were going to hurt me or my children for what he was making me do. He just laughed and said they would not be stupid enough to mess with me. But at one o'clock the next morning, I woke up to the sound of pounding on my door. It was two of the insurance agents. And when I refused to open the door, they yelled and threatened me for what I had done to them, warning that something bad was going to happen to me. I went to work the next day and reported this to the police and the investigators. They told me the men were just scared and making idle threats, but they would not do anything. When I started receiving threatening phone calls throughout the night, I changed my number and even had it unlisted.

I tried to quit my job, but they threatened that if I quit before the investigation was over, I would be charged as an accessory to the crimes. Then I would be arrested, and my children would be taken from me. I called my attorney and made an appointment to see if they could really do this. But once they found out about the appointment, they would not let me leave work. When I did not show up or call him back, my attorney came to the insurance office. The police officers cracked the door just enough for me to speak to him. But because they had informed me that one of their colleagues was on the way to get my kids, I had to tell him I no longer needed his services, and they closed the door and locked him out. From that day forward these men held me against my will and forced me to work unreasonably long hours and days on end.

My kids and I were forced to move into the motel for about a week where the private investigators were staying. Our room was adjourning theirs, and I had to keep the door between us unlocked. My sons, upset by the turmoil, were not sleeping well, and their teachers reported that they were very upset at school and were saying they just wanted to go home. I told the investigators and the police that I needed to take my kids home. They agreed under the condition that an investigator would stay overnight in my guest room until this investigation was over.

I knew they did not trust me and expected me to leave town. But I agreed so I could take my children home. They needed their own beds and their toys. My autistic son needed his regular routine, or he would start acting out again. I was miserable. I was not used to anyone staying in my house, and I wanted my life back. I was sick of all this insurance mess and scared every day for me and my children.

I could not understand why they were doing this to me and had not involved Ellen who had been there over ten years and had to know a lot more about this mess than I did. I finally asked Mike, the lead insurance investigator, why. He explained that Ellen had been there long enough to be involved and until we ruled her out, they did not want to scare her off. He said millions of dollars had been paid out over the last several years, and he needed to be able to find it. I had been there the least amount of time, and even if I had been involved, I could not have had enough time to embezzle that much money.

Claims were filed on homes, chicken coops, automobiles, and other small structures. Paint and body shops in town were involved. Crooked contractors out to make a buck were involved. This is how it worked: the insured would file a claim. Their agent would go out and look at the damage and approve their claim. The body shop or the crooked contractor would submit a bid inflated way above cost. The insurance adjustor would approve the bid, as he had the final say, but he did it at a price. He was paid off the top. Whoever did the work was paid, and then the agent and the insured client got a percentage for filing the claim. Everyone walked away happy with money in their pocket. This is what the insurance agency manager had been trying to prove for years. All I did was help to expedite this investigation when I learned what to look for and what agents were involved. There were only two in the office that played no part in the fraud.

The next day after work I told the investigators I needed to buy groceries before I went home, and I needed some time before one of them came to spend the night. They agreed. But as I left the parking lot, I felt ill at ease, as if someone were following me. And sure enough, a carload of men was on my tail, trying to push me off the road! I recognized a couple of the men from the paint and body shop where I had taken pictures earlier. They kept motioning for me to pull over, but I refused and made it to the grocery store, where I jumped out of the car and ran into the store to find the store manager. I told him I was being followed and was scared. He walked to the front door with me, and when I pointed out the vehicle parked beside my car, they quickly drove off. He promised to watch for them, and when I finished shopping, he walked me to my car, saying he would stay until I got on my way. However, when I tried to start my car, it was dead! The manager opened the hood and discovered that a carburetor wire was missing. He called the police while I called the insurance company office. The police came and made a report, and the insurance company called for someone to fix my car.

From that day forward, my mobility and freedom were further restrained to the point where I could not travel without an escort. Now the investigators knew they had put me in harm's way, and they had to protect me. I wanted to see my dad who was in the last stage of lung cancer, but an investigator had to go with me. My dad did not like this arrangement, but he wanted me to be safe. I did not even have free access to make or receive calls. The investigators put their recording on my home phone, and I was not allowed to answer it. Anyone who called had to leave a message, and several left threats on my phone. I hated it! All of it!

One Monday morning after arriving at work, a bouquet of flowers was delivered to my desk. The card read, "Who knows what tomorrow holds in store for you?" The police investigated, but the order was placed over the phone, and a cash payment was dropped off by a little boy. There was no way to trace any of it.

The next day I was fitted with a wire under my shirt and sent to a meeting with a woman I knew. They believed she was involved in this insurance scam, and I was instructed to act like I was helping her and warn her about the investigation. But the goal was to get her to admit to what she had done. I got her on tape admitting to receiving a lot of cash from the insurance adjuster. I did not realize they would be using this recording at a later date to bring charges against this lady.

The next morning, I was told to come into the office earlier than usual to meet with some insured customers. I usually took the boys to school, but it was too early that morning, so the investigator stayed at my house to get the boys on the school bus. But as I was driving down the dirt road from my house, I heard a loud BANG! Glass flew all over the back of my head and down the collar of my shirt. OMG! I had been shot at! The back door window behind me had been shot out. Had it been seconds earlier, the bullet would have come through my window, and I could have been shot in the head. My kids are usually in the car. If they had been with me this morning, one of them could have been shot! This was it! I was done! I turned around and drove back home, too scared to think. The investigator called 911, and the sheriff came. Too late; whoever did it was gone. I refused to go into the office that day and kept my boys home from school. And the investigators relented, realizing I was in no shape to work. Meanwhile, at the office another bouquet of flowers arrived with the card, "Today is your lucky day!" When they informed me, my nerves were shot, and I could not stop crying.

The next morning, I was told I had to go to work, so I got up and got my boys ready for school. And this time I was glad the investigator was there because I had been scared all night. But when we walked outside to get in my car, all four of my tires were slashed! The tow truck came and took my car to town, and the insurance company paid for four new tires to be put on my car. Once I got to work, the police and investigators decided it would be a good idea for me to leave early that day. Whoever was doing these things knew my schedule – when I left home and what time I got back. They decided that I would leave the office that day around 4:30 to vary my schedule. The agency manager and another agent, Robert, agreed to stay at the office until I called to let them know I was home safe.

When I was close to home, I noticed that a small truck in front of me moved into my lane and was heading straight at me. As it got closer, I recognized that the truck belonged to one of the insurance agents. OMG! Three of them were in there, and they were not getting out of the way. I swerved off the road, into a ditch, and ran up under a barbed wire fence before I could stop the car. I got out and tried to run, but two of them caught me while the other one got back in the truck and drove off. They grabbed my arms and dragged me through the barbed wired fence, not caring that it cut my leg up. I lost a shoe in the briar patch under the fence, and they kept dragging me, yelling at me, calling me a bitch and a snitch, and telling me they were going to teach me a lesson for ratting on them. I was crying and telling them I did not do that, and that the investigation had been going on for years. But they would not listen.

They just kept dragging me through the underbrush and briars. I begged them not to hurt me because my babies were at home and needed me. They said I should have thought about that before I started helping in this investigation. We finally came upon a clearing back in the woods where the other agent was standing beside the truck.

They pushed me down on the ground and pulled off my remaining shoe and pantyhose. One of them slapped me and kept yelling at me for turning them in to the insurance investigators. They each took their turn with me, raping me as hard and brutally as they could. Because of the stench of alcohol on their breath and the torture they were putting me through, I started throwing up, and that made them mad. They grabbed my arms and dragged me over to the truck, pulling down the tailgate and throwing me over it onto my stomach. Each one of them raped me again from behind until I was lifeless. I couldn't fight them; my body would just not move anymore. Then they pushed me off the truck and into a fire ant bed and jumped into the truck and drove out the back of the woods. I was hurting so badly; I barely felt the ants crawling over me and stinging me everywhere, but I did manage to crawl out of the ant bed, rolling over and over in the dirt and grass to get most of the ants off me. I had no shoes, and my dress was shredded by the barbed wire and the briar bushes. My one foot was full of thorns from being dragged through the woods, and my body ached everywhere.

All I could think of was that I had to get home to my kids. Did the babysitter stay with them or were they home alone? The question with no answer gave me the strength to get up and start moving. I did not know that she had called the office when I did not arrive home and had not called her. One of the agents answered the phone and told her I had left over an hour ago. Then he and the agency manager jumped in their car and started driving on the route I would have taken home. About 3 miles from my house, they found my car off in the ditch and up under the barbed wire fence. They got out of their car and started yelling my name. It was faint, but I could hear someone, so I started screaming and screaming until one of them found me. He picked me up and carried me out of the woods to his car. He called 911 for help, but over and over, I begged him to just take me home. I had to find out if my babies were safe. He finally agreed to take me home if I went to the hospital later. Once we were home and I discovered that my babysitter had stayed, and the kids were fine, I refused to go to the hospital. I was home at last, and I could not bear the thought of anyone else touching me. The pain was simply too great.

For the next week I was at home with my boys, although not alone. Two of the private investigators stayed at my house. One slept in my son's bedroom, and one slept outside in his car. They promised to keep me safe this time. But after that week off to recover, the private investigators forced me to continue assisting with the investigation. This was never going away! It took well up until the Christmas holidays to gather all the evidence needed to file charges on all the individuals involved. This case would be heard in the Federal Courthouse in Danville, Virginia.

On New Year's Eve at the office, there were only a few of us left, after they had terminated four of the employees, but we decided we wanted to meet somewhere and celebrate the New Year. We all needed some fun. The whole office had been under so much stress. It was agreed that we would meet at a place called County Line Dancehall, a club just outside of town. I had to be escorted by an investigator, but that was fine with me. I was scared to be alone, especially after dark. We all had fun. We danced and cried for what we were going through and made New Year's resolutions for a better upcoming year. After celebrating and bringing in the New Year we all said our good-byes and left. Escorted by the investigator, we picked up my boys from the babysitter on the way home since I had not felt comfortable with her watching them at my place at night.

Once home I put the boys to bed and went to bed myself. About 3:30 am, I heard a loud banging at my door. The investigator heard it as well, and we both went to the door to find two highway patrolmen standing there. When I opened the door, the officers introduced themselves and showed us their badges before asking me if I was Jennifer Reed, the lady who worked at the insurance company. I said yes. He asked me if I worked with a lady named Ellen at the insurance office. Again, I said yes. He said there had been a terrible accident, and Ellen was deceased. He needed me to go to the city morgue with them and identify the body before he contacted her children. Ellen was a single mom of three teenagers. OMG! What happened? Who did this?

I had met all of her children, but I told the officer I did not want to do this. My boys were asleep in their beds, and I was not going to wake them. However, the patrolmen would not take no for an answer. They told the investigator to stay there with my children and gave me no choice but to ride with them to the city morgue. After arriving there, the examiner came out to explain to me why Ellen's body looked the way it did, trying to prepare me for what I was about to see. Her vehicle had run off the road on the river bridge right outside of town and had flipped over before going into the river upside down. Because the temperature was around 20 degrees, she had frozen, and her body was blue.

It was horrible! It was so hard to look at her, but I had to do this for her kids. I told the Highway Patrol it was Ellen, but I had to get out of there. Never would I do this again. I had seen stuff like this on TV but never the real thing. Who did this to her? Was it the same men? Was Ellen involved in all this and knew too much too? So many questions raced through my mind.

It got more frightening when the police report came back. After pulling her car out of the river, the investigators found paint on the driver's side of the door, indicating that her car was forced off the bridge into the river. An investigation was started but never came up with anything. I will never know what Ellen knew about all this insurance fraud, but it was apparent that her life was taken because of it.

For the next couple of months, I was the only secretary left in the office to do everything. It was busy, but that helped keep my mind off things. The police department pulled out of the investigation, leaving only the International Insurance investigators there to wrap up the case. We wanted to interview for another secretary, but we did not want to bring anyone else into this mess until it ended. I could not leave because they needed me. My father was not doing well at all, and I went home on the weekends to spend time with him. The threats were finally behind me.

> Beneath many strong, independent women
> lies a broken little girl who had to learn how
> to get back up and trust in God that her life
> would change for the better.

4

DEATH...
DRUGS...
SUICIDE...

On Mother's Day 1991, my father lost his battle with lung cancer, and I was devastated. Not only did I lose my dad, but I lost my mentor, the one who helped me conquer it all, and I could not imagine what I was going to do. After his funeral, my mom begged me to sell my house in Marinette and move in with her. She was not a strong person, and she had the responsibility of caring for my dad's eighty-two-year-old mother who had been living with them. Mom was only fourteen years old when she and my dad married, so he was all she knew, and she kept telling me she could not go on without him. Plus, she feared for me and my kids because of all I had been through. So, under the circumstances of my father's death and the finalization of the fraudulent insurance investigation, my resignation was accepted, and I was free to move on. I did not even wait till my house sold. I looked forward to this transition, feeling that for once in my life my kids and I would be safe. Little did I know how trouble would follow me to my hometown.

It started off wonderfully. My boys went to the same small country school that I attended as a child, and they loved it. They got involved in sports and became popular at school. I was company for my mom and became my grandmother's caregiver. Since I received unemployment benefits from the insurance company, I was able to stay home for a while and watch over everyone. Best of all – I felt safe!

Mom was doing well also, but as the holidays approached, she became very depressed – not eating or sleeping and losing weight quickly. I tried talking to her, but by this time I recognized that she needed professional help. I asked her to make an appointment with her family doctor to see if he would prescribe medication to help her through this challenging time. She agreed and followed through but did not get the kind of help I was expecting. Instead, the nurse called in prescriptions for any medication Mom asked for if she slipped her cash. Mom received pain killers at one pharmacy and valium at another. She even got a prescription for my dad's medication he took for the extreme pain he experienced with cancer. My dad was dead! What was this nurse thinking? Did she need money that badly? I could not imagine what her motive could be for doing this to my mom, who could barely function under the influence of all these drugs. She slept far too much, and it was extremely difficult to wake her when she passed out. I called the ambulance on two separate occasions when I could not awaken her. They would take her to the ER and pump her stomach.

I was devastated and did not want my boys to see her like this, so I went to my brother for help. But he told me to leave her alone – to let her grieve however she wanted. He was not concerned that she might overdose. When I went to my attorney for help, he called the doctor's office and reported the nurse, and we thought the problem was resolved. But no. The attorney called me on a conference call with the pharmacist a few days later. The pharmacist told us he could not believe my mother was still alive with the mixture of drugs she was taking. He said we had to find her help. But when

I went to my brother again, he still refused to get involved. The doctor did terminate the nurse, and the local pharmacies shared the information and became extremely cautious about supplying Mom with medications.

But she became upset with me for interfering with her medicine. And although I tried to reason with her and explain the pharmacist's warnings, her mind was not right. She ended up taking matters in her own hands by frequenting the bar where my brother spent most of his day and becoming friendly with one of his friends who was into drugs. Then she was able to buy all the illegal drugs she wanted and down them with alcohol. After that she met a man, and all they did was sit and drink while she popped her pills and began going downhill fast! My hands were tied. She would not listen to anything I said. No one – her grandkids, her mother-in-law, nor I – mattered to her anymore. Instead, she asked me to move out and take my kids and grandmother with me so her new boyfriend could move in. This was not my mom! The drugs and alcohol had turned her into a woman I had never known.

When Mother's Day was only two days away, I sat down with her and asked if we could go away for the weekend. I told her I would find someone to stay with my grandmother because we needed to get away, pointing out that the pills were making her depression worse. And although she was reluctant to go anywhere, she apologized and said she was sorry she had gotten mad at me and that she knew I was trying to help her. For a minute there it was like I had my mother back, but later that evening she was back to her beer and the pills.

The next night around 9:00 pm, I noticed that she went out to sit on the rocking chair on the front porch. I left her alone for a little bit because I knew the next day was Mother's Day, and I was sure she had my daddy on her mind. Every time I went to check on her, she would assure me that she did not want to come in then but would be in later. I could tell she was getting agitated by my checking on her, so I told her goodnight and took the boys to get them ready for bed. She assured me she would come in soon and would call me if she needed me.

I fell asleep, and about 5:00 am I heard the front door close. When I got up to check, she was coming into the house after being out there all night. I asked if she was okay, but all she said was that she was going to bed. I went back to bed too. It was too early to cook breakfast because my grandmother and the boys were still asleep. Around 8:30 or 9:00 am, I heard the cartoons come on, and I knew the boys were up. I told them I would make breakfast after I checked on my grandmother. I found her sitting in her chair crying. My dad was her only child, and this day was going to be hard for her. I told her I was making her favorite breakfast – homemade biscuits and gravy – and would be back when it was ready. Then I tiptoed down the hallway to my mother's room to see if she was up. When I found her lying in her bed wide awake, I bent over and kissed her on the forehead and said, "Happy Mother's Day." I told her I would get her when breakfast was ready. She seemed fine and said she would get up in a minute.

I went into the kitchen and started making the biscuits. The boys continued to watch cartoons and were just asking if it was ready when I heard a big POP! My mom's TV was old, and sometimes it popped loudly, so I walked over to it and asked the boys if the sound came from the TV. When they said no, I went down the hall to check on Mom. I realized that she was in the bathroom and the door was closed, so I called her name and asked if she was okay. She did not answer the first time, so I asked her again. Then I heard her cry, "I can't see!" I tried to open the door, but it was locked. So, I ran and got the key that she kept in her dresser. The boys sometimes locked themselves in there, so we made a key. Unlocking the door, I went in and screamed as loudly as I ever had. There was my mother standing at the sink facing the mirror with blood running down her head and arm. She was holding a .22 pistol and had shot herself right in the temple. I tried to grab the gun, crying, "What have you done?"

She kept screaming, "I can't see! I can't see!" and was waving the gun around, pulling the trigger over and over. Bullets were hitting the sink and the wall. I was astonished at my mom's strength. I could not get the gun from her hand.

My boys ran in to see what was wrong, finding me wrestling with her trying to get the gun while bullets were flying. I had to let go of her to grab the boys and get them out of there! I did not want them to get shot! I shoved all the boys out the door and right into my grandmother as she was coming down the hall. I had to get all of them out of there. Once I got them out, I closed the door and turned to get the gun, but my mom turned it to her heart and pulled the trigger, falling to the floor! I was in total shock, but I remember screaming for the boys to call 911 and my brother. I fell to the floor, embraced my mom, and prayed someone would get there in time to save her. We were both covered in blood. After that I could not move or speak. I do not remember who got there first. All I can remember was my house flooded with people and police officers while my mom, my life, was dying right in front of me. Someone disentangled us, walked me into the living room and sat me in a chair. My boys ran to me and jumped into my lap. I will never forget their faces. They had seen their grandmother shot and covered in blood. How could their minds handle this? I understand that someone took the boys off my lap and out of the house – I do not remember.

A day or two later we had to go to the Justice of the Peace for the inquest. I rode with my brother and his wife to attend the meeting. The judge asked if we had any questions or concerns about our mother's death and assured us that he was there for anything we needed. He had been one of my dad's good friends, and he knew we were going through a grim time. When he asked if we wanted to order an autopsy of the body, my brother said there was no need. He knew our mother was depressed and was satisfied that she had committed suicide because she could not handle losing my father. I agreed as well. If my mom had drugs in her system, I did not want it to be known. We wanted to protect hers and dad's name in our little community where they were dearly loved. We buried my mom soon after and tried to go on the best we could. My boys were very hurt. I had to take James to his psychiatrist, as he was so distraught from what he had witnessed and needed medication to calm him. Autistic children cannot handle the level of trauma he had experienced. Besides James, I still had my grandmother to care for, and the devastation from losing her only son and now her daughter-in-law in this manner had drained her will to live.

Not long after mom died, the insurance company's attorney called to let me know it was time to begin preparing for the upcoming federal court trial where I would appear as a witness against the men charged in the insurance scandal. I was still reeling from the trauma of my mom's death, and now I must face in court the men who had raped me. (This trial was not for the rape but for all the money they had swindled out of the insurance company over several years. The rape trials would come later.) Would I have the strength to sit in the same courtroom with these men? I was not sure I could do this, but I knew I had no choice. My attorneys recommended I see a psychiatrist in Danville to help me make it through the trial. I saw her several times, and she prescribed a medication called Prozac. I felt nothing out of the ordinary for a couple of weeks, but then I started to feel crazy. I would start driving somewhere and end up going the opposite direction from where I was supposed to be. I just did not feel right, and when I thought of Mom and all the drugs she had taken and how she did not seem like my mother, I determined that I was not going to do that. I was not going to be this crazy person I felt I had become. I decided I would handle this on my own – with no drugs!

I had to be there in seven days. I went to the mailbox one day and there was a letter. No return address. The letter warned me that I better not show up for the trial or there would be consequences. Where did this come from? Who knew my address? And how did they find me? I left no forwarding address when I moved. I was overcome with panic! Not again! I could not handle this again. I raced to my attorney's office with the letter. He called the sheriff's office and made a report, but the letter was impossible to trace. He advised me to be careful, aware of my surroundings, and not to leave my house unless I had someone with me. I was scared. How could I do this again? For the next several days I stayed at home with my boys and my grandmother, but I did not get a lot of sleep. I heard noises and had bad dreams.

Finally, the day of the trial arrived. I got up early, as I was going to meet with my attorneys and ride with them. My grandmother was so scared she begged me not to go. I got the boys up so they could get ready and get on the bus for school. I told them goodbye and walked out the door to my car. OMG!! All four tires on my car were flat! Not only mine – but my mom's and my grandmother's cars all had flat tires! They had all been slashed. I ran into the house and called my attorney who called the sheriff. They had to drive me to court, and hopefully we would not be late. That made it all the harder to sit in the same room with the men that had raped and terrorized me. I never made eye contact with them and did my best to act like they were not even there. I made it through that day and saw that legal action would be taken against them. I was done!

After that trial was over, I decided to file a suit against the insurance company and the international insurance investigations firm for putting me in "harm's way" during the entire investigation. I hoped this would give me closure for all the pain and put all the bad experiences behind me. I just wanted my life back and my boys to be able to live normal lives. I knew I would never be the same again, but I was praying we would all get through this.

But not long after the lawsuit began, so did more trouble. The private investigator from the international insurance investigations came to my hometown and hunted my family members down. I will never know how he convinced my brother to even talk to him, but it was his wife who agreed. She never liked me, and this was her time to shine. She would do whatever she could to make my life miserable.

During this time, my grandmother fell, broke her hip, and needed a total hip replacement. At eighty-three, she had to go into a nursing home for physical therapy after her surgery to learn to walk on her leg again. However, she laid in the bed too long, caught pneumonia on top of the emphysema she had suffered with for many years, and passed away in the nursing home. This was the third death in three years, and losing the three people I was closest to was devastating. It was so difficult to plan another funeral for my family. It was all I could do to just get through each day. But I had a reason to keep going on – my boys! I had to be strong and not allow them to see all this hurt I felt inside. I fought off depression each day as hard as I could.

Months went by, and the suit against the insurance company was going well. Then one evening when I was outside watering my flowers, a constable from the county pulled into my driveway. Curious, I walked over to him as he got out of the car. He handed me an envelope and stated, "You have been served."

"Served? What for?" I asked. He told me to take the subpoena to my attorney and let him take care of it. So, the next morning I went to my attorney's office, and we read the subpoena. It was a summons to the Grand Jury. My brother was accusing me of my mother's death. He was saying he believed it to be a homicide, not a suicide. What? My heart sunk to my knees. Me hurt my mother? After all that I had gone through to try to help her, had he lost his mind? What was wrong with him? The drugs and alcohol had taken a toll on his mind.

My attorney answered the subpoena that commanded my boys and me to appear before the Grand Jury. How could my brother put my boys through this? Didn't he know they had suffered enough? My attorney advised me to stay away from my brother, but how could I? I went straight to his house to confront him. Someone had put him up to this, and I was going to find out who. He walked out on his front porch when I drove up and told me to get back in my car and leave or he would shoot me for trespassing. I begged him to talk to me and all he said, "You better go while you still have the chance." I was devastated. This was my brother, my own flesh and blood. We had been through so much by losing mom, dad, and our grandmother. How could he do this – especially to his nephews?

Over the next few weeks, things deteriorated. The Greenville Enterprise, our local paper, and all the newspapers in the surrounding towns printed my picture connected to my mother's presumed wrongful death. They reported that I had been subpoenaed to the Grand Jury for formal accusation. My life crumbled. My boys came home from school crying, telling me all the mean things the kids were saying to them at school, and saying they did not want to go back. I had to rush James to his psychiatrist for medication to help him gain control since he was not handling the situation at all. My heart broke as I sat down with my boys and told them that people like to gossip. This was all a lie, and they knew it. I reminded them to stop and think back to the day this happened. I hated having to bring these horrific memories back up, but I needed to make them strong so they could handle all the mean things people were saying. They knew what happened. They were there. The people were just talking about things they did not know, and they were not there, or they would not be saying a word. I encouraged them to just be strong and tell the kids they did not want to talk about this because it hurts too bad and walk away. I said, "Remember, you were there." I also tried through my attorney to get James out of having to testify to the grand jury because with his mental status I did not think he could handle it. But I was informed that it would be impossible to exclude him. The Grand Jury wanted to hear his story of the day his grandmother died.

My brother went first and came out fifteen minutes later. I was next. My account took a little longer, as I cried a lot having to relive the day and retell exactly how it happened. I was allowed a lot of breaks to regain my composure, and they were very understanding. Caleb, my youngest, was next. He was in there for about fifteen to twenty minutes also. He came out very teary eyed and upset. He ran directly into my arms and was shaking badly. I hated my brother for this. He was standing in the hall and saw my son's reactions. They saved James for last. After about thirty minutes, I was worried. Forty minutes passed, and I was a mess. I looked at my brother and burst out crying. I could not imagine how James was holding up in there, and I was hurting imagining what he was going through. Forty-five minutes later, the door opened, and James came running into my arms, shaking and terrified. But my attorney assured me that he had done an amazing job recounting the events. James stutters when his anxiety level is high, and he simply needed to repeat many things over and over. But it was done, and we could go home. As I walked by my brother, he would not even make eye contact with me.

We would have to wait a day to know the verdict, and the wait seemed endless. My whole life and the lives of my sons were in the hands of those twelve members of the Grand Jury. I knew the truth of my mom's death, and my boys knew the truth, but would the jury know? If indicted, I would go to jail, and what would happen to my boys? I could not bear to even think about it. It all seemed like a bad dream, but it was not. It was REAL!

My attorney called me around 3:00 p.m. the next day – the longest day of my life as I waited to hear that verdict. I prayed and begged God to take care of me and my boys – not to allow me to be taken from them. Finally, the verdict was in – it was "no billed." This meant that there was not enough evidence to support a criminal charge against me. God is so good! He knew the truth, and he held my hand through it all. I sat the boys down and told them. They were so excited, but they quickly asked if the kids at school and all the newspapers would quit saying mean things about me. I told them some would, and some would not. I had to explain that this world is full of mean people, and you cannot stop it all. I told them if anyone said anything to them just to tell them to find out the truth before they said anything. But hopefully, our lives would somehow return to normal with less chaos. And over the span of the next couple of weeks, James improved. We were doing therapy with his psychiatrist once a week, and it was helping. That was the key!

My lawsuit against the insurance company ended with an undisclosed amount of cash. They did not want any of this to go to court.

Dear God, thank you for always
walking beside me and holding my hand.

5

AUTOMOBILE ACCIDENT... EXHUMATION...

Months went by and all was fairly quiet. The newspaper articles slowed to a trickle once the Grand Jury results were released. So those who had avoided me when all of the chaos started began talking to me again, and the kids at school almost stopped saying mean things to the boys. Life was getting so much better, or at least I thought!

One Saturday evening, we invited our neighbors over to swim, and while we were all outside in the pool, my home phone started ringing over and over, but never long enough for us to get to it. And because it was the old rotary phone we had back in the 90's, there was no way to see who had called. Both the kids and I kept running in trying to catch the call, but we missed it again and again.

Finally, it rang when I was inside, but when I answered, my heart stopped. The caller, from Mother Theresa Trauma Hospital in Anderson, Texas near where my oldest son had gone to visit his dad, informed me that my son, Thomas had been in a major automobile accident, and had been life-flighted there, since it was the hospital closest to the scene of the wreck. All the caller would tell me was to come quickly, that he was in bad shape, and that they could not make any promises that he would be alive when I got there. I called his dad and learned that our son had massive head trauma and had died twice – once at the scene of the accident and again on the helicopter – but they were able to resuscitate him. My younger sons and I packed quickly and left for the hospital. It was 9:00 pm, and we were at more than three hours away. I remember being terribly upset, having to drive for hours without knowing if he would even be alive when I got there.

I had no cell phone in those days, so there was no GPS. All I could do was follow the map to Anderson and look for the hospital once I got there, recognizing that time was not on my side. We finally arrived at the hospital at 1:30 am and went straight to the ICU. The doctor came out and told me that we needed to see him and say our goodbyes. He did not know how my son had held on this long, and he did not expect him to make it through the night. We all rushed into his room, without the thought that it would not be good for James to see his brother in this shape. All I could think of was just getting my hands on my son! It was a horrible sight, and James had a total meltdown. Thomas was connected to all kinds of tubes and was almost unrecognizable with his swollen head and his left eye hanging out of place. I had never seen anyone look like this. James and Caleb burst into tears, and I knew I had to get them out of his room. I did not want to leave, but we could not stay there.

We camped out in the ICU waiting room that night. I felt that I could not leave the hospital in case we lost him. I just wanted one more word, one more kiss from my son. But the morning came, and he was still alive. The doctor said it was a miracle and it was most certainly God's work. That is all it could have been. For the next three weeks, as Thomas remained in a coma, his dad and I rotated shifts so that someone would be there at all times. Not long after, we started noticing that my son's eyes would twitch, and his fingers would move when he heard us talk. The doctor explained that he was trying to wake up from the coma, but he was just not sure when or if he would. He suggested pulling out the life support because in some cases when the patient was not fully comatose, that action would trigger a response, and the patient would wake up. His dad and I agreed, since we were assured that if he did not wake up, the life support would be put back in.

I waited outside the doorway as they began the procedure to remove the tube, and when I heard a scream, I knew he was awake. Soon the nurse came out to tell us that they had to restrain him because he woke up mad and had begun to pull out his IVs. He had actually slugged the orderly who was trying to help him. She assured me that I could see him, but only for a few minutes. They were going to move him into a private room soon where he would be restrained until he calmed down.

Thomas did not recognize me or his dad for a few days. His memory would come and go, and the doctors explained that this was a common occurrence. I will never forget sitting in his room with him when he asked me to put the hospital telephone where he could reach it. I asked him who he was going to call, and he said, "I am calling my mom, Jennifer Reed. She will come and get me out of this hospital." I started crying as I realized that he did not know he was talking to his mom. I handed him the phone, and he proceeded to dial but got very frustrated at it.

The doctor called me aside to tell me Thomas had two severe brain bruises that needed to be removed surgically. I had never heard of removing bruised parts of the brain, but this was a head trauma hospital, so I trusted that they were doing what needed to be done. He explained that the bruises were causing pressure on his brain and that pressure was the cause of his acting the way he was. His dad and I agreed to the surgery, and it was scheduled for a few days later. When the day arrived, I was very nervous and unsure of the outcome, not knowing if it would help him or if he would ever be normal again. But it took a few hours, and the doctor said all went as planned. We would just have to see when he woke up what his reactions would be after the pressure was removed.

The next day he could not move his hands or his feet and could not stand alone. I had to feed and shave him. He could chew his food and swallow, but that was all. We were informed that now we needed to transfer him to a rehabilitation hospital. We could not simply wait to see what would happen to his body. He needed therapy immediately to regain the use of his limbs. So, he was transferred that very evening. The rehab was very hard on him, and he was highly agitated at times when he could not do what he wanted to do. But he had some of the best therapists in the world, and they worked wonders with him. He began to remember little things. His long-term memory was better, but he had no short-term memory of recent things that had happened, like the accident.

I traveled back and forth to the rehab and watched my son get better and stronger every day. He wanted to come back home with me once he was discharged, but I told him to go to his dad's house first so he would be close to the hospital, just in case something happened. Then when the doctor released him to go out of town, he could come home with me. And in about 6 weeks, he was discharged. He was up walking and had even given a speech to the patients in the rehabilitation hospital. He wanted them to know they could do anything they set their mind to. He was a big inspiration to many because of all the obstacles he made it through. He was definitely a miracle – God's miracle!

While I was running back and forth to Anderson to care for my son, the International Insurance Investigator was busy in my hometown. He was not happy that my lawsuit had settled in my favor and had come to my hometown to stir up problems for me, trying to discredit me anyway he could. He went to my brother's house – and instead of running him off as he should have – my brother made friends with him and bought into the notion that it would be a good idea to order the exhumation of our mother's body. This was when I found out that this insurance investigator was the reason my brother had taken me to the Grand Jury over my mom's death in the first place. It did not seem to matter that the Grand Jury had "No Billed" me on the indictment or that it had been three years since her death. I could not imagine what my brother was hoping to gain or what the investigator had promised him to make him do these crazy things to my family.

I received a phone call from my attorney who informed me that the private investigator had gone to the Danville County Courthouse and called a news team for a press release, telling the media that my brother was still not convinced that my mom's death was a suicide and that he had recommended that her body be exhumed. He was making my life miserable for sure. Things had really been rough with my son's wreck and now this? I told my attorney that under no circumstances would I agree to an exhumation of my mother's body – not for my brother and definitely not for this insurance investigator. She had been buried three years ago, and there was no way I would consider disturbing her remains.

The newspaper articles started slamming me relentlessly, accusing me of having an affair with the Justice of the Peace who had performed the inquest and inferring that I had influenced him to rule my mother's death a suicide. They splashed pictures my brother had provided of me alongside pictures of the Justice of the Peace on the front page of our local paper and those from all the surrounding areas. The stories portrayed us as having a romantic relationship and stating that he had strong feelings for me and was trying to protect me. One article clearly stated that if I had nothing to hide, I would agree to exhume my mother's body. This was insane! People in our community were talking again, and so-called friends once more decided they wanted nothing to do with me. The kids at school were saying things to my boys, and little James was having to go through the drama once more. It was so unfair.

Weeks went by and the investigator did not give up. He uncovered the fact that my neighbor was a county commissioner and was respected by a lot of people in our community, so he and my brother went to him for his help. This commissioner was good friends with the DA at the courthouse, so they felt that if anyone could push this exhumation through it would be the DA. This commissioner had been good friends with my mom and dad, and his wife and my mom were good friends, so I was shocked to learn that he had gotten involved in this scam. I thought he was smarter than that and wondered at first what he hoped to gain. But soon I realized that he would be running for office again soon. It was apparent that politics is the name of the game.

One morning there was a knock on my front door, and I opened it to find Channel 19 and their news team standing on my porch. Cameras started rolling, and the reporter asked, "Why won't you exhume your mother's body? What do you have to hide?"

Without a reply, I slammed the door in their faces and went straight to the phone, called my attorney, and said, "I cannot take this anymore, and neither can my boys! How can I make this stop?"

My attorney took a deep breath and said, "Jennifer, if you will exhume your mother's body, you will prove your innocence, and this will all go away."

I agreed and told him to please call the DA and get it done. I could not take any more chaos. I had one son at home laboring every day to heal from his automobile accident and get his life back while two more sons were having to endure their lives thrown into turmoil. We were all tired of this nightmare.

My attorney called back a few days later to let me know that the exhumation was scheduled. He gave me the date and time, but I could not bear to go watch them dig up her grave. My poor little momma had been there for three years, and this was insane. I chose to stay home until it was removed. The body was exhumed and taken to the Pogue County Medical examiner in Boles, Virginia, and it would be several days or maybe a week until we knew the results. The wait would be horrible for me and my boys. It was the longest three days. Then the call came from my attorney with the results. It was ruled a suicide by the medical examiner just as it had been by the Justice of the Peace in my county during the initial inquest. I was promised that my mother's body would be taken back to the cemetery the next day and put back where had originally lain.

I called the Greenville Enterprise and the other newspapers that afternoon and asked them to please get the report from the medical examiner's office and publish it. Some agreed that they would, while others did not reply at all. Only trash sells papers. I knew that if it had been ruled a homicide, I would not have even had to ask. I found out the hard way that media loves trash, and they love to trash people. The Greenville Enterprise posted a very small notice near the last page of their paper, so tiny that you would not even notice it if you were not searching for it. I called the reporter who had trashed me so often in her reports, but she declined to talk to me. I wanted a front page. I deserved it, but no one complied.

But finally, my mom's death and her body had been put to rest. At least that was what I thought. Three days later, as I was driving from Danville to Sterling on Highway 19, I decided to stop and make sure that my mom's grave had been put neatly back in place. But that was not what I found. I saw the hearse and several cars near her grave and jumped out of my car heading to her grave. The funeral home employee met me about halfway telling me that I really did not need to come any further. I did not understand, and I did not stop. I asked, "What is going on? I thought my mom's body had been put back a few days ago." He explained that it was supposed to have been, and they were there trying to figure out what had happened. My dad's grave had been there since 1991, and my mom's had been there since 1992. This was 1995, and when they dug up my mother's remains for the exhumation, they discovered it had been in the wrong place.

Upset was not the word! I wanted to know who was responsible for this catastrophe. Well, well it turned out that my neighbors, the county commissioner and his wife, were in charge of the cemetery. They were the ones who sold the plots and were responsible for the cemetery's upkeep. I had no idea what I should do. I knew that if I were to go to him in person, there would be trouble, and I was not about to cause more harm to myself and my family. The commissioner was so busy in politics and in snooping in everyone's business that he could not even do his job right. I immediately left the cemetery and went home to call my attorney. I knew he would take care of this. It turns out the cemetery thing was a mess. Mom's and Dad's plots were in the wrong place, but they could not move them because there were other people on either side of them all the way down. There were no other spaces available, and there would have been a lot of upset people if they had to start calling families and moving plots. It was decided that they would put my mom's remains back where they were and just leave it alone. Of course, the county commissioner did not get cited or anything for this. He had friends in high places. The publicity would not have been good for his upcoming election. Needless to say, things were swept under the rug. Case closed. Maybe he would leave me alone now.

At least the news media left me alone. They had no trash on me now, so I was no longer of interest to them. I learned from my attorney that the investigator had told my brother that if I had been found guilty of having something to do with my mom's death, not only would I face charges, but I would have lost the home mom had left me in her will. My brother would have ended up with the homestead Mom and Dad had left to me. Finally, I understood his motivation. Death in families often bring out *greed*. It certainly did in my family.

Not long after this, my attorney called again to inform me that my brother was at it again, and I was sure the investigator was again the instigation. He had accused me of spending all my grandmother's estate. My grandmother had given me the Power of Attorney, and I took care of all her financial needs. Because of his accusations, I had to do a discovery dating back three years on her finances. This took a great deal of time and caused a lot of headaches working with the banks and getting all the cancelled checks, but I got it done. I proved that there was not any money to be shared with him. Her finances only took care of her and paid for her caregivers. It was just enough to cover her costs until she died. He had never helped me with her while she was alive. I had a hard time just getting him to come over and see her.

You had better watch those people that bounce back
from everything that was meant to destroy them!
Those are God's people, and they are not
to be played with!

6

AUTOMOBILE ACCIDENT... LIFE FLIGHT...

For the next couple of years all was quiet – no media hounding me, nothing my brother could think of to sue me for – and the international insurance investigator had left town because everything he turned up proved to be false. No one was interested in hearing his bullshit anymore. Caleb and James were doing great in school, and Thomas was pretty much back to normal with only a few issues. It was a Sunday afternoon, and I was a work at the Junction Hill Restaurant – a day I will never forget.

I received a phone call that Caleb and James had been in a major auto accident on the way to town. One was in the ambulance headed to the nearest hospital and the other was waiting for life-flight to land and transport him downtown to the medical center. I dropped the phone and ran out the door. I had to get to the scene – a good twenty minutes away! But by the time I got there, both the helicopter and the ambulance were gone, so I first drove into town to the nearest hospital. I could hardly drive I was so upset. NO! Not again! I prayed and prayed they would be okay.

When I got to the hospital's emergency room, I found James on his way to the x-ray department with multiple lacerations. I called Thomas and a friend to come be with him so I could get to the medical center. All I knew about Caleb was that he had been pinned under the steering wheel, and they had to use the Jaws of Life to get him out, so his condition did not sound good. Another friend came to the hospital and insisted on driving me to the medical center, and thankfully I accepted. I truly was in no shape to drive. I was crying so hard I could not see the road.

Once we got to the hospital, Caleb was in the ICU and had been diagnosed with multiple lacerations and internal bleeding. The doctors were considering removing his spleen if the bleeding didn't stop, so they were waiting to see how he would fare. Meanwhile my oldest son called me to report that they were discharging James, and he was taking him home. That was a great relief.

But a couple of hours later Thomas called me back, saying that James was in severe pain and could not walk. Now, James never complained about any kind of pain, so I knew he was hurt. I asked him to bring James to the emergency room at the medical center where I was at. And when they arrived an hour and half later, the ER checked him in and went to work on James immediately. Besides the lacerations we knew about, he had a broken nose, a broken foot and five broken toes – wounds our local hospital did not even notice. They just sent him home! So, they checked James into the hospital with plans to keep him comfortable and repair his injuries the next day.

As I waited, I had to ask myself if I had the strength to handle all of this. Yes, I would find it. Had I been through worse? Yes, I knew I had. I kept telling myself that we would survive.

> The hardest thing to do is swallow the hurt,
> carry the pain, tuck it away, and wait.

A couple of days passed, and Caleb's internal bleeding slowed, so they agreed to move him into the room with James so I could be with both of them since we needed to remain a few more days. Once the internal bleeding stopped, I knew there would be no surgery, and within the week they were both discharged. When we arrived at home, we discovered that the community support was outpouring. My house was full of friends with all kinds of food. The boys' friends were over, and it was hard to get a minute's peace, but I was thankful that my boys were loved by their school and our community.

I did lose my job at the restaurant because they were short staffed and had to hire someone immediately when I told them I would be out for a while. I understood. It was nothing new. I had been without a job many times by now.

I discovered that Caleb had fallen asleep at the wheel as the bright morning sunshine glared through the window. He apparently had stayed up too late the night before. His truck was totaled, but one of the ladies he hit head-on was in critical condition. She fought a long hard battle to survive. Her insurance company sued mine, and when we went to court, they won the case. I was afraid Caleb would lose his license, but he did not. He was the star running back on the football team that year, but the doctor told him he could not play for a least a year because he needed more time to heal. He explained that one hard hit to the stomach would send his spleen back into a bleeding stage again. So, time went by. The boys healed, and I was out looking for another job.

It was the summer of 1999. Caleb was working at Brookshire Brothers, and James was mowing and weed eating the football fields and around the outside of the school yards, working through a high school summer program for those with special needs The coaches were great with him and taught him a lot of life skills. I got a job in town at a Healthcare center, and things were going well.

Then one day I got an emergency call for Jennifer Reed. I said, "This is she." The caller told me that there had been an accident at the high school, and James was waiting on the life-flight helicopter to be transferred to the medical center. I said nothing. Not again! I dropped the phone again and took off running, yelling to my boss that James was in a bad accident. When I arrived at the school, James was in an ambulance. They were waiting on the helicopter, but his leg was inside an inflatable device because of a compound fracture with the tibia and fibula protruding from his skin. The bleeding was pretty severe, and they needed to get him to the hospital quickly.

The coaches were crying as they tried to explain what happened. The paramedics explained that James was in shock, but I was amazed when out of the blue he said he was hungry and asked me for his lunch box. Clearly, he was in such a state of shock he did not even feel his pain.

The life-flight landed, loaded him up, and took off. I called Caleb at Brookshire's to come ride with me to the hospital. By the time we connected and got to the hospital, James was in preliminary surgery to clean out the dirt that had been embedded in the wound from the accident. They had to prevent infection. After they finished cleaning it out, they brought him into a private room, and several doctors came by to explain the long surgery scheduled for the next morning. They would put a rod in his leg to replace the shattered bones. Then they would have to do a skin graft from his thigh to cover up the big hole left on his leg and take muscles from his abdomen to replace the damaged leg muscles. OMG! This was so much to absorb. Poor James had no idea what he faced. He was calm as they administered pain medication and managed his Autistic meds.

The doctors warned that there was no guarantee the skin graft would work. They would put a cast on his leg with a small opening so they could check on it at night with a flashlight, since it could not be exposed to the light. The surgery would involve six different surgeons and would take about eight hours because of all the complications, but they promised to send a nurse out hourly with a report so I would know he was okay. This was very scary. I prayed that James would be okay both mentally and physically. He had endured so much the previous few years, and I was really worried about him.

When the morning came and they took him into surgery, James was cheerful, with no pain or any idea of the adventure that lied ahead of him. I chose not to even try to explain anything other than that they were going to fix his broken leg. A nurse did come out every hour with the report that he was doing great. My only concern was that he was under anesthesia for so long, but they assured me he was fine.

And after eight hours and twenty-five minutes, it was done; he was headed to recovery where I could soon see him. By this time there was a waiting room full of my friends and James' school friends. I was definitely glad for the company. Soon I was able to visit him in recovery, and then we went to his room where he barely woke up during the night despite the constant visits from doctors and nurses checking on him. "Everything is fine!" they would say.

The next morning before daylight, the doctors started coming in with their flashlights inspecting his leg to assure that the skin graft was taking. Seven long days passed, and James was tired of his hospital bed. He was ready to get up and wanted to go home. I kept inviting his friends to come see him and keep his spirits up. School was about to begin, and it was his senior year. He was worried that he would not be able to walk. I told him that at first he would not, but soon he would. But by day ten, the skin graft did what it was supposed to do, and we could go home.

He could not put any weight on his leg for six weeks, so he went home in a wheelchair with instructions to keep his leg elevated above his head. We had to hang a hook over his bed with a sling for his leg. What an uncomfortable way to sleep. In order to take a shower, his brother and I had to wrap his leg in a garbage bag and carry him to the bathroom. If that was not bad enough, he was especially unhappy about starting his senior year in a wheelchair, but that was his only choice. After six weeks, when the doctor released him to start therapy, James was excited but so surprised at how weak he was when they got him up to walk. He thought he would simply stand up and walk! He worked on walking for six weeks, and all his friends were so helpful when he was at school. They pushed him in the wheelchair and carried all his books. He was a popular item for sure. He soon graduated from the wheelchair to a walker, which he hated. He still had to continue therapy, and we ran back and forth to the doctors. We even rented a wound pump to help promote his healing.

The school year went as well as it could with his disability. He soon graduated to a cane, and by graduation he was able to walk across the stage and receive his diploma! What a guy! With his autism, James was a trooper. I do not think I would have handled all this as well as he did. Both James and Caleb graduated in 2000, despite all the obstacles they had to overcome. I am so proud of my boys!

I put the home place up for sale because I had decided that I did not want to live around the corner from my brother any longer. I had only stayed long enough for the boys to finish school and had planned to leave afterward. I could not stand to drive by his house and hated to see him drive by mine. What he had done to me and my kids was unforgiveable!

I looked at my past, and I realized it was God
who had blessed me and my family and kept us alive.

7

SUICIDE...
LOSS OF JOB...
GRANDCHILDREN...

In a few months, the healthcare facility where I worked announced they were closing their doors. Medicare had come out with new standards and would no long cover our services for the elderly, and it was mainly the elderly who came to us for help. Here again I was on the search for a job. Been there, done that! It felt like my life was a never-ending freight train on a circular track!

I had planned to sell the house anyway, so I knew we were moving. A friend who was employed at a big hospital in Boles, Virginia, not far from my hometown helped me land a job there. We sold the home place to some friends and moved away. Caleb was going away to college, and I was able to get James a job at the hospital where I worked. Things were good. I was away from my brother and from the people who still loved to gossip about my mother's death. Those were all mainly my brother's friends anyway. I loved my job, and James was happy too. We went to work every day together and then went home. We went on little mini vacations and spent most Saturdays at the movies. Life was good.

Caleb's grades at college began to suffer because he was partying a little too much and working a lot. He called one day asking to move back home with me and James. I agreed but told him he would have to get a job or go to school where we lived. Instead, he joined the Marines, and I was happy with that decision because he needed the discipline. Going off to college in another town had not worked, and I knew the Marines would give him the direction in life he needed. He went to boot camp at Camp Pendleton, and James and I flew there after six weeks to watch him graduate. He would serve one weekend a month at the Reserves and had decided he wanted to become a paramedic. I told him I would help pay for the training, and he planned to get a part time job for his spending money. He went to school and finished as an EMT. An ambulance service soon hired him and put him to work as he continued his schooling until he became a paramedic. I was proud of him.

A few months later, Caleb's life begin to spiral out of control. He was involved with a married woman that worked on the same ambulance. She became pregnant and claimed it was Caleb's, although she was still living with her husband. Rebecca divorced and then married Caleb. That was when another kind of nightmare begin. After my granddaughter was born, she ended up living with me because Caleb and Rebecca fought continuously and separated very soon. Rebecca managed to get pregnant again and once again claimed it was Caleb's. So, we all rented a house together for me to be there to take care of both babies. However, it was total chaos. They fought all the time and were very ugly to me and James. Rebecca moved out and left me with both babies. James could not take the pressure and begin acting out.

I decided to rent a nearby apartment so I could be there as needed but still have a peaceful, quiet place for James. But the move and the pressure of everyone fussing at him drove James to attempt suicide. He tried to shoot himself with a gun, but thankfully, he knew nothing about guns and did not recognize that I had it on safety. So, he got a steak knife and cut his stomach, pulling the knife downwards after nicking his diaphragm. The wound was not life threatening, but I was devastated. I called the ambulance, and he was rushed to hospital. They stopped the bleeding, but due to his mental state, we had to admit him to a psychiatric hospital where I could only see him certain times during the week and on the weekends. I blamed myself and thought I would lose my mind. I was in a painful dilemma. I needed to care for him in a quiet, loving home without all the drama of my other son's relationship, but I also needed to raise my grandbabies.

It was not long before the marriage ended. I came home from work one day to find my son with my six-month-old grandson and two-year-old granddaughter on my front porch. Caleb told me he could not take care of these babies and work as a paramedic. My daughter -in-law had gone back to her second husband who had her third child. So here I was, trying to work and raise both grandchildren. Both parents continued to keep them on their days off but were quick to give them back once I got home from work.

I was not aware that Caleb was also having problems with his duties as a Marine. Apparently, his personal life was affecting his attitude in other areas. One day, two Marine officers came to my job to tell me that he had gotten in a fight with his drill sergeant and was no longer welcome at the reserve. If he went there again, they would arrest him and throw him in jail. They asked me to get all his Marine gear together, and they would come back to the hospital in three days to collect it. Again, if he did not comply and give it to me, they would arrest him and throw him in jail. What in the world? He had told me he was serving one weekend a month. Instead, he was not showing up for duty, and when his drill sergeant approached him about the matter, it got physical, and my son beat him up badly. I could not believe Caleb was acting this way! His personal life had taken a toll on him. I was at a loss. I wanted to help him, but he had gotten in over his head this time with the Marines, and there was nothing I could do. They threatened to give him a Dishonorable Discharge, but luckily, he came out with an Administrative Discharge.

About six months after I took the babies into my home, I lost my job. Our company was taken over, and the new owners brought in their own employees. Thankfully, I was offered a severance package and unemployment benefits since I had been there for twelve years. I took it and told my son we needed to rent a house together to raise these babies. He agreed. We rented a home big enough for all of us, including my special needs son. I was concerned about returning to the chaos, but since it was only us – the ex-wife was not going to be living there –the drama should be limited. At least that is what I thought!

Everything went well for about the first six months. And since their mom did not come and get them a lot, I was like a second mom to my grandchildren. The new problems began when my son started bringing other women into our home at night. If it had been only one, we may have been able to work something out, but it was several. I put my foot down and told him it had to stop. He said, "Okay, it will. I will get my own apartment and move out." And that was exactly what he did, leaving me with his children in the big house that I could not afford on my own. I had to find a smaller home for me, James, and the kids. He would come on Saturdays to see them, and their mom would come off and on to take them for the night. I had to get on food stamps to feed us, as there was no financial help from either Mom or Dad. I will never understand how a mother and father could not want their children with them all the time. I didn't raise my son like this. I am not sure what their mom's excuse was, but I knew her life stayed in complete turmoil, so the kids were better off with me.

James had been doing a lot better since his suicide attempt now that we were living without his brother's chaos. He still struggled everyday with the grandkids around, as they required so much of my attention. We were no longer able to go and do the things we used to. I assured him they would grow up soon, and maybe their dad or mom would someday grow up and want their own children back. I was not holding my breath though. They still had a lot to prove that they were ready to be parents.

James loved the computer and spent a lot of time on it. But when I came home early one day, I was shocked to see sheets tied together and stretched out along the floor leading to his room. When I checked on him, he was sitting in his computer chair with the last sheet tied around his neck. I screamed and quickly untied the sheet from around his neck, asking him, "What in the world is wrong with you? Who upset you?" I discovered that this was the day Robin Williams had killed himself by hanging himself with bed sheets. James had understood that Robin was very upset and unhappy, so he thought that since he had been unhappy this last year, he would hang himself too!

I immediately called the psych hospital where he had been before, and they came to get him. I was told that this attempted suicide was not a suicidal ideation as the first one was. This time he was just more curious to see if he could accomplish it. He loved Robin Williams. He watched all his movies and was very sad that he had died. James had to do therapy for a couple of months until he promised all the psych team that he would never do anything like this again. I thought I had seen it all, but I could only imagine what would have happened if I had not come home early. Would he have carried out this dreadful attempt? I just thanked God that I was there in time.

As time passed, things began to improve. My grandkids were maturing and were doing well in school. I worked at their school, and James found a job at our local grocery store. Their dad would visit on Saturdays – and their mom when she chose to. I never understood this. I was their grandmother and could hardly stand for them to be gone one night from me. We were very close. I was their grandmother, their mother, and their father all in one. Their mom married two or three more times during this time, and their dad had multiple girlfriends. I hated that my grandkids were subject to so much turmoil in their lives, but we held on strongly to each other for comfort.

Finally, their dad met a lady he cared for a lot. They dated about four months before they decided to move in together. I warned them that it was not going to be easy, because she had two children, and I could see jealously among the three youngest. One of Sara's kids was in high school, so he did his own thing and was not a lot of trouble. But her little one was only a year older than my grandkids and was very jealous. He could not stand for my grandkids to get attention from his mother. But my son just wanted to take his kids back after they had been with me for five years. I told him it was not going to be that easy. He could just not take them. We needed a transition period so they could get used to living with him again. He had not lived with them, only kept them a night or so on the weekends. He did not believe me, but he soon saw that it was the best way to get them back.

So, James and I moved in with him and his girlfriend until I could find a mobile home to put on their lot. It was the best thing for the kids. Both my son and his girlfriend were in the healthcare field, and they left at 5:30 in the morning and returned home between 7:30 to 8:00 each night. I got all four kids up and ready for school, drove them to and from school each day, fixed dinner, and prepared them for bed by the time the parents came home. I was with my grandkids again all the time, and I loved it. But Sara became jealous. My grandkids wanted me to do everything for them, as I had always done, and she did not like that. She wanted to be the one they came to. However, she made no effort to show special attention to them. She had her own small son and spent all her free time with him. There was no doubt he was her favorite, and she made no attempt to hide it. I soon realized I had to get out of that house.

Finally, after three months my new mobile home arrived. My son and Sara had purchased it for me, and I paid half the mortgage so that I could be available 24/7 to take care of the kids. I moved in as quickly as I could and still walked over every morning at 5:30 to wake the kids up and get them fed and to school. Then, after work I would stay until 8:00 or so every night when one of them came home. My grandkids would walk me home every night, begging to stay with me. They sensed how Sara showed favoritism to her son and not them, so they clung to me. I hurt for their pain and tried to talk to my son, but all it did was get my grandkids in trouble. So, I had to stop. He lived there, and he knew it, but he would not do anything about it. She was the breadwinner of the family, and apparently, the money meant more than the happiness of his own children.

After I moved out, Sara would take her son special places on her day off and send my grandkids to me to keep. And when they would go home at night, they would learn that she had taken him out to eat and bought him toys. He enjoyed showing them to my grandkids to make them jealous. This hurt deeply, but my son would not do anything. If I said anything, I would have to leave, and I did not want to leave my grandkids to be raised in that environment. So, I catered to the parents and showed extra love to the children the best way I knew how.

Things only got worse as time progressed. The kids did not want to stay home, so they would stay with me all weekend. Sara complained to my son that she would never bond with the kids as long as I lived next door to them because they would not stay home with her. She never tried. She would send my grandkids to me so she and her son could go do things together. Then he would always come home with something new, and my grandkids' feelings were hurt. Her son's closet was full of new clothes, and he had five or six pairs of tennis shoes to choose from daily. My grandkids did not even have enough jeans or clothes to make it through the week without washing them on Wednesday! And Lord forbid if they asked for a second pair of shoes. I know my son saw this. I was madder at him for allowing it. What was wrong with him? And he treated her like a queen.

In 2019, James and Caleb's dad, my ex-husband, passed away. My grandkids were not even allowed to go to the funeral, and it was their grandpa. Sara's son did not know him, so I guess that was why none of the kids got to go. Unbelievable! Caleb and James went to the funeral together, while I was told to take my own car. This was Caleb's doings. His wife was slowly turning him against me.

When the will and estate was ready to be distributed, Caleb was the executor, as James, being autistic could not handle any type of business transactions. But Caleb would not give James his part of the estate. My son and I fought over this daily. His rationale was that since James was autistic, he would not know what to do with it, so he did not want to pay him what he was owed. I had James' POA and insisted that he be given what his dad left him in the estate. Caleb refused, saying it was their dad's money – not mine.

One day, he brought over the taxes owed on his father's land and a copy of the bill for the headstone that was finally placed on his dad's grave, insisting that I pay for it. I told him when he put James' money in his account, these items would be paid. He got mad and told me he was taking back the truck he had given me to drive. And he did just that. I found myself without transportation and had to borrow money to make a down payment on a vehicle so I would have a way to work. I still cannot believe he did that to me. The grandkids had been riding to school with me each day, and he stopped that too. Either he or Sara took them to school. But I still had to bring them home. And I had to find my own transportation to do that.

When Mother's Day came, I got a text from Caleb that my present was on the BBQ pit outside if I wanted it. I never saw anyone that day, not even my grandkids. My heart was breaking. How could my own son be so mean to his mother?

COVID-19 hit, and Sara and Caleb were the first ones to get it in our family. The grandkids went to spend the weekend with their mom as to stay away from home. But when they came home on Sunday, they informed me that their mom had COVID, too. Wow! It seemed like it was everywhere. When we went to school on Monday morning, I had to tell the principal and the school nurse that we all had been exposed, and they made us go back home. This was the first big break-out, and you were required to quarantine for fourteen days. Caleb was furious that I had told the school. But I had to – I worked there; I was not going to lie.

He called the school and cursed out everyone he talked to, saying they had no right sending his kids home for quarantine as I was not their parent and should have never told anyone they were exposed. He told them when he got over COVID, he would come up to the school and settle with all of them. He said I had no right to disclose such confidential information, and someone would pay. And he did exactly that. He showed up at the principal's office and tried to get me fired. When the principal told him she would not fire me, as I was doing what I was supposed to do as an employee, he was furious. He went to the Administration office and tried to get the principal fired because she had refused to fire me. I was so embarrassed. This was my job, and he was totally out of control and upsetting everyone I worked with.

One Saturday morning, I got up early and sat on my couch to wait and see if the grandkids were coming over. I decided to look at Facebook until they woke up. As I scrolled down the news feed in Facebook, I saw a mobile home for sale. It looked like mine! OMG!! It was mine! I recognized the flowers and pots in my yard. I called my son and asked him what in the world was going on. I had been paying half of the trailer note for the past five years, and he never mentioned selling! I asked, "Why are you selling the house out from under me and your brother?" What son would throw his mom and special needs brother out on the streets? I was devastated. I learned that Sara's best friend was a realtor, and she and Sara took the pictures one day when I was at work. Then the realtor posted them on Facebook! I knew she did not like me, and I knew she was at the root of the problem between me and my son.

A couple of Saturdays later, I was at my granddaughter's softball game and my son called me on my cell phone to inform me that I had to be out of the trailer in three weeks, as they had sold it and would soon be moving it off the land. I asked him, "Do you really want to throw your mom and special needs brother out on the streets? What was wrong with you? How could you let some ungrateful woman come into your life and mistreat your mom and your kids?"

He had no reply other than, "You had better find you a place to go!"

I went on Facebook and posted that I was the owner of the porches on the mobile home. I had worked and paid for them myself. If anyone wanted them to please contact me. They were not for sale with the trailer, and they were not my son's porches to sell. A very sweet lady from the nearby church came and bought the porches, paying me cash for them. She had to find someone to detach them from the mobile home and move them for her. It had been raining every day for a week, so I assured her that the porches were hers, and she could get them when she could.

I informed my son that the porches were paid for, and the lady would get them picked up as soon as possible. James and I had found a house to rent not too far from the school where I worked. My principal and other families came and helped us move. They even brought some of the football team, and we were all moved out and settled in our new home in three hours. Amazing! I saw that day that friends can love you more than family.

A week later, my neighbor who lived across the road called to tell me she saw a truck hauling my porches down the street with my son's truck following. I immediately called him, but he just laughed, saying they were not my porches anymore because I had moved off and left them. I had no choice. I could not let him do the lady that way, so I went to the constable in our area and told him what my son had done. He paid Caleb a visit and told him he either had to give the woman the porches or pay her money back. She did not want the money; she wanted the porches she had bought. But Caleb insisted that she take the cash. When she told him he needed a lot of prayer, he laughed in her face. Later, I found out that the porches had been sold to Sara's best friend's grandmother. So, this was her doing again.

I had also left my portable building on the property because the movers had to wait until the ground dried from all the rain. We had tried, but got it stuck and buried deeper in the ground. When I called my son a week later and told him we would be moving it now that the ground had dried, he posted a "No Trespassing" sign on the driveway and threatened us not to enter the property. Again, I had to get the constable to talk to him. I got my portable building against his will. He had lied, saying it was his, but I had the receipt to show that it was mine.

Within a couple of weeks, Caleb and Sara sold their home and moved to another town. My heart broke for my grandkids. I did not know if I would ever see them again. I had raised them from babies, and they missed me as much as I missed them. How could a father be so selfish and hurt his own kids?

My grandkids called me every day whenever Caleb was not home. They missed me so much and were having a hard time adjusting to their new school. They would text me at night after they went to bed. My heart was breaking. Finally, they got to come and stay with me one weekend. My son made me drive out there to get them and take them home, but I would have gone to the end of the earth to be with them.

Strong women are not born, they are forged
in the fires they have had to walk through.

8

ALCOHOLISM... BROKEN FAMILY TIES... INSPIRATION...

Thomas, my eldest, continues to drink and suffers from alcoholism. He started drinking at age 21. I felt sure after his bad wreck with the brain surgery he would stop, and he did for a short time, but has continued now for many years. Now he is 50 years old and could not stop if he wanted to without professional help. His drinking has caused many problems in our relationship to the point that we do not have one anymore. As we all know, an alcoholic is never wrong and takes no blame for their actions. I have backed away after he sent me a text telling me I had ruined 48 years of his life. That knocked me to my knees. I do feel that the chaotic life he was raised in was partly to blame for his drinking. **But I cannot say** that if I had to do it all over again it would be different, because the many life traumas I faced were not invited. **Neither can I say** that time heals all wounds, because the memories will always remain. I have been living with my memories since I was seven years old.

Caleb chooses to continue living his life without his mother. Maybe his traumatic childhood lies somewhere in the back of his head, and he too holds me responsible. His life has been a mess, and he has been lucky to get away with some of the things he has done in his life. My grandson comes and visits me every now and then and tells me how much he misses me. He would come more often, but it upsets Caleb, and there is always some type of consequence he faces for coming. My granddaughter will not come because of the things Caleb has told her about me.

James is doing well. His autism affects him in his adult life differently than when he was a child. However, he has held down the same job for eight years. He still lives with me and always will until I am no longer in this world. I am sure his mindset was affected by all the trauma that we experienced in the past, but he handles it better than his brothers have. He is the sweetest, and he would never treat his mother as they do. He is very loving.

LOVE was the beginning of all my problems as a child. I did not understand what real love was, and I believed all who told me their version of it. Love is not just a feeling; it is a choice we make every day to treat others with kindness, compassion and understanding. True love is not about possession; it is about acceptance. It is not about what we receive; it is about what we give.

I took a job at our local school, working with the special needs students. My heart was big for them, and I had plenty of love to give. Having raised my autistic son, James, I learned how to communicate and develop a bond with these students. They know when they are loved, and they all became a piece of my heart. I knew I was in the right place, and I knew I was an inspiration to the students.

I also work part-time with the elderly people who either have no family or have a family that does not have the time to take care of them. I am a blessing to them as much as they are a blessing to me. These individuals are losing their independence and must depend on others. It is so scary for them, and they feel so alone in this world. I am thankful that I can be there for them. They thank me every day for the love that I show them.

Sometimes I inspire my patients
but most of the time they inspire me!

Life is like a book. Some chapters are sad, some are happy, and some are exciting. But if you never turn the page, you will never know what the next chapter holds. I have no idea how many more chapters my life will turn into. When you want a different life for yourself, you have to start moving differently. Old keys do not unlock new doors.

I am on a journey to inspire others who have similar circumstances, different traumas, or just have the need for someone to take their arm and tell them things will be okay. God is closer than you think. All you have to do is talk to him. He will lead the way. It may be a long journey as mine was, but he will walk with you every step of the way.

I hurt every day for my two sons that I do not have a relationship with anymore. I pray every day that God will open some doors.

Step into my shoes and live the life I have lived.
And if you get as far as I have,
just maybe you will see how strong I really am.
God did this.